ZANZIBAR STONE TOWN
an *architectural* exploration

Text by Professor Abdul Sheriff
Photographs by Javed Jafferji

Published in 1998 by
The Gallery Publications
Zanzibar

First published in 1998 by
The Gallery Publications
170 Gizenga Street, P. O. Box 3181, Zanzibar, Tanzania
gallery@swahilicoast.com
Also at:
32 Deanscroft Avenue, Kingsbury, London NW9 8EN,
United Kingdom

© 1998 The Gallery Publications
Text by Professor Abdul Sheriff
Colour Photographs by Javed Jafferji
Edited by Graham Mercer
Illustrations by Abdul Basit, Bayuu and M. Ausy.
Design & Dtp by X Press Design (T) Ltd.
Printed in Singapore

ISBN 9987 8877 24

Acknowledgements
Publishers are thankful to Zanzibar Archives for their help.

CONTENTS

A roofscape of Zanzibar. During the nineteenth century many of the houses had flat stone terraces, but the heavy rains played havoc with the mangrove poles supporting the roof. The houses were thus capped by roofs of corrugated iron sheets in various colours of rust, or red Mangalore tiles from India, giving the modern roofscape its distinctive hues. To the left of centre is the Anglican Cathedral with its single spire.

CHAPTER 1

The Stone Town:
an *architectural* synthesis

The name Zanzibar has such a romantic and exotic ring to it that some visitors and enthusiasts are easily led to a comparison with 'the ancient Baghdad of Haroun el Rashid'. From a distance, the whitewashed buildings of the Stone Town of Zanzibar apparently dancing on the waves of the Indian Ocean may well raise great expectations.

But Zanzibar is not a copy of Baghdad: if it were, why not see the real thing?

*Sailing to Zanzibar.
The Indian Ocean dhow,
with its typical lateen sail,
more than anything else,
expresses the essentially
maritime culture of the
Swahili people of the East
African coast, linking them
with other peoples around
the Indian Ocean.*

*Narrow streets are typical of
the Stone Town. The
various stages of
discolouration and decay of
the lime-washed walls, and
the different shades of
sunlight trying to
penetrate the lanes make for
a painter's paradise.*

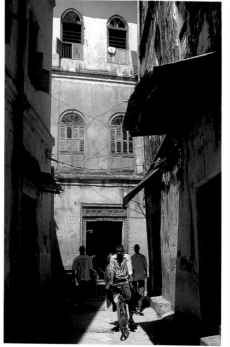

Zanzibar is Zanzibar. Not many minarets pierce the sky, nor do domes characterise its skyline. But it is no less fascinating. It is a unique architectural synthesis on the East African coast of a couple of millennia of interaction between Africa and the lands across the Indian Ocean.

Speaking of the East African coast in the second century A. D., the Periplus, a Greek navigators' guide, mentions;

Arab skippers and agents who, through continual intercourse and intermarriage, are familiar with the area and its language.

Oral traditions of the Swahili people are

replete with stories of migrations of people not only from the African mainland, but also from Arabia, the Persian Gulf, India, and even beyond. They represent a heterogeneous society in a constant process of homogenisation. The cosmopolitan character of the people of the coast is fundamental to a consideration of their cultural heritage. Nowhere is the cultural synthesis so visible as in the architecture of Zanzibar.

The Stone Town is an agglomeration of various of architectural traditions from the East African coast and the world of the Indian Ocean. The Swahili people have been

A view of the town from the top of the House of Wonders looking south, with the Old Fort in the foreground, and the double spired St. Joseph's Roman Catholic Cathedral to the extreme left.

An aerial view of the Stone Town from the south. The Stone Town stands on a triangular peninsula with the point at Shangani at the extreme left, and the base along the old Creek which ran diagonally to the right. The Creek has now been filled up. At the centre right is the House of Wonders.

A coffee seller, making the rounds with his brass coffee pot and charcoal burner. Nowadays they are more likely to be found at the popular intersections where men meet and share cups of coffee.

experimenting with available building materials, notably coral stones, lime, mud and mangrove poles, for more than a thousand years. They have developed a technology on the East African coast itself, although they have never hesitated to accept new inspirations and make them their own.

In spite of different influences, the simplicity of the design, the limited variety of building materials available and the homogenising hand of the local master craftsman (*fundi*), have resulted in an harmonious unity within a picturesque framework. While different features are distinguishable, they now constitute a single common architectural tradition that is uniquely Zanzibari or more broadly Swahili.

The Stone Town consists of some 2,000 stone buildings, organised in named quarters or wards (*mitaa*), such as Mbuyuni ('at the baobab tree,') Soko Muhogo ('cassava market',) Hurumzi (after the Persian Gulf island of Hurmuz), which have greater social and topographical significance than the streets which dissect them.

These wards are bound together by an intricate network of narrow streets and lanes which are intimate, allowing neighbours to gossip and exchange recipes from one window to another above the busy streets. Many lovers have thus exchanged their glances, words of passion and, as in the case of the nineteenth century Princess Salme, even marriage vows. The broad canopies that almost touch each other provide shade to passers-by. It is possible to walk from one

end of the town to another except at high noon without having to brave the hot sun.

The Stone Town is also bonded together by a large number of social nodes, such as mosques, *mikahawa* (coffee places) and *barazas* (lit. stone benches, i.e. meeting points). Islam requires its followers to say prayers five times a day in a neighbourhood mosque, which brings the community into constant interaction. Zanzibaris typically while away the time, in the late afternoon, and between evening and night prayers, at the *barazas* or coffee places, relaxing and exchanging information and views. Such social interactions bring a degree of intimacy that is typical of Zanzibar and the Swahili towns.

The Stone Town is more than meets the eye.

When it rains in Zanzibar, it pours, and the streets become rivers. The cleaning of the drainage system should solve the latter problem, but the former is part of Zanzibar's natural heritage.

The Stone Town is quite comfortable with its past. It is cluttered with graveyards, often surrounded by a low wall. In a very congested town, they could be the green open spaces if they were cleaned and planted with trees without sacrificing the santity of the graveyards.

CHAPTER 2

The *Swahili* Roots

The town of Zanzibar began as a typical Swahili settlement, perhaps as early as the tenth century, although most of the existing buildings date back to the nineteenth century. Its roots may lie in a fishing village at Shangani, and as late as 1823 there was a clump of huts and a mosque there. However, because of constant erosion, the original site was already several metres under the sea by the time Burton visited the town in 1857.

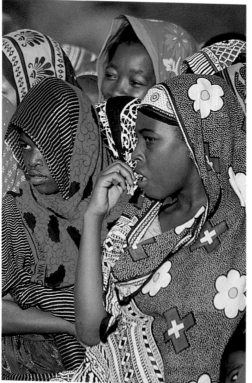

Sometime in the seventeenth century Zanzibar town became the capital of Queen Fatma who ruled over the indigenous people of central Unguja. Her palace was on the site of the House of Wonders and the Old Fort. She was on good terms with the Portuguese who built a chapel and other houses to the south. She was succeeded by her son, Hasan, who is said to have done much to clear the bush on the peninsula on which the Stone Town now stands.

The town was also settled by immigrants from Hadhramaut in the Yemen. They included the Alawi clan who married into the local ruling family and became the Mwinyi Mkuu (Great Lord) rulers of Zanzibar. They were settled in some of the oldest parts of the town in Kajificheni, and were associated with the Forodhani Mosque, the earliest of the existing Friday mosques in

Zanzibar town.

They were accompanied by Swahili families from other parts of the coast, such as Faza and Malindi on the coast of Kenya who established quarters which were sometimes named after their original home towns. They built some of the earliest existing mosques in the town, such as the Malindi Bamnara mosque whose unique minaret, dating to the seventeenth century, shows close similarities to those of Chake Chake on Pemba, Mbaraki and Shela on the coast of Kenya, and some mosques in Hadhramaut.

These settlers perpetuated the Swahili planning and architectural tradition that is seen most fully developed in the Lamu archipelago. The Swahili house was designed as an inward looking self-contained complex organised around an 'intimacy gradient' from the semi-open entrance porch, the characteristic *daka*, where male members of the household received most of their guests for a cup of coffee and sweetmeat (*halwa*), through the courtyard, and into the parallel living rooms which become darker and more intimate the farther they are from the courtyard.

Swahili houses were normally plain on the outside. However, there is a photograph in the Zanzibar Archives of a house in Baghani which had unusual external stucco decoration that does not seem to occur in the Lamu archipelago. The interior of Swahili houses, on the other hand, were usually elaborately decorated with intricate carved coral or plasterwork. It increased in intricacy as one moved across the house from the courtyard

The Swahili dress betrays a great deal of its oceanic heritage. The turban, long white kanzu and an overcoat, bushti, (see page 12) had become standard dress of the male elite of the society, while the black veil which covers the whole face except for the eyes is typical of traditional Swahili female costume The women wear the colourful kangas that may have been inspired from as far a field as Indonesia.

Zanzibar at the beginning of the nineteenth century was a typical Swahili town. It was located on a peninsula that was almost completely cut off from the main island of Unguja except for a narrow neck of land at the southern end. The central part was built of stone, but it was surrounded to the north and south by mud & thatch huts, already extending across the creek to the east into what became Ng'ambo ('the other side').

Swahili graves were similarly decorated with stucco work, and sometimes with inlaid chinaware, as in this grave at the bottom. Unfortunately many of these plates have been stolen or broken by insensitive marksmen.

The Swahili had developed an indigenous architecture over more than 1,000 years, using local raw materials, coral stones, lime, mud and mangrove poles. It was characterised by a notched arch and intricate stucco work generally over the inner walls, but sometimes even on the outerwalls, as in this old photograph. Only a few of the Swahili houses now survive in the Stone Town.

to *ndani*, the master bedroom. It was probably the most elaborately decorated in the house, with almost entire walls covered with panels or wall niches *(zidaka)*. Even the toilets had lavish ceilings, plasterwork and arches.

Since houses were grouped in *mitaa* originally occupied by kin groups, and consistent with the Islamic desire to maintain privacy for the womenfolk, many of these houses were linked above the street by covered galleries *(vikio)*. They enabled the women to move from one house to another without having to come down to the street. Such galleries linked the many buildings in the Palace complex on the seafront during the nineteenth century, and some of them survive to this day.

Throughout the nineteenth century many porters, artisans and other urban workers also lived on the peninsula on which the Stone Town is located, although by the end of it a large working class quarter had emerged across the Creek in Ng'ambo. They lived in wattle and mud huts with pitched thatch roofs and a ground plan that seems to be a modification of the old Swahili houses. From the entrance porch, with a raised platform on one side, where minor trading or artisanal work was carried out, a passage led to the open courtyard that had been shifted to the back of the house, where many of the household chores were carried out. The long parallel family rooms were now formally cut by a central corridor. In due course some of these huts on the peninsula were converted into single-story stone houses to accommodate

Intricately carved wooden beds, high enough to allow another person to sleep beneath them, are celebrated in some of the earliest surviving Swahili poetry, common in both Swahili and Arab households in the nineteenth century. The floors were often covered by Persian carpets. The marble-top tables were introduced from Europe later in the nineteenth century.

poorer inhabitants of the Stone Town.

Typical Swahili houses were more widespread in Zanzibar Town until the beginning of the nineteenth century. Economic expansion and large-scale migration of Omani Arabs and Indians during the nineteenth century gradually overwhelmed the Swahili architectural tradition. Swahili-type houses were transformed or replaced by others that betray new inspirations. Today a few traces of the Swahili roots of the Stone Town still exist in the older central and northern parts of the town.

Swahili architecture was also expressed in elaborate graves, though many have been demolished or lie buried under bush or heaps of refuse. Although Islam frowns upon elaborate mausoleums, man will not be restrained in his quest for eternity. Some Swahili graves show intricate carving of coral and plaster that match any in their houses. Others were inlaid with imported Chinese pot-

tery, which unfortunately became favourite targets for marksmen and bounty hunters. Some of these graves also carried elaborately carved coral tombstones with lines from the Qur'an around the panel and information about the dead in the centre.

The Arab dress varied from the elaborate costume "of the raling elite to the simple 'Kanzu' and 'Kofia' of the ordinary people".

a) Sultan Seyyid Bargash in full regalia.
b) Princess Salme in her traditional costume and jewellery.
c) Arab woman wearing the veil
d) A typical Omani youth wearing an "gaal" headdress and robe.

CHAPTER 3

Elegant *Arab* Simplicity

In 1699 the Portuguese, who had dominated the East African coast for a couple of centuries, were finally driven out by a combination of Omani and Swahili forces. The Portuguese chapel and the house of a Portuguese merchant were incorporated into 'a ridiculous little fort' that now forms part of the Old Fort on the seafront. This marks the beginning of a new phase in the architectural development of the Stone Town.

The Old Fort, built in the early eighteenth century by the Omani Arabs after they had driven out the Portuguese. It was variously used as barracks, prison and a railway yard. The gatehouse was demolished at the beginning of the twentieth century to allow the train to pass through. After the rails were uprooted, the gatehouse was recostructed in the old style, and the Fort served as a Ladies Club. It is now one of the Stone Town's Cultural Centres.

Beit al-Sahel, the Place by the Sea, on the Zanzibar sea front was the town palace of the Sultans. The simple long building on the left was typical of the early Arab architecture in Zanzibar. In the 1870s a pavilion was added jutting out from the palace, which served as the reception area. Behind it stood the lighthouse which was damaged during the 1896 bombardment and was demolished.

The Omani Arabs came as merchants, plying their wares in dhows which sailed with the monsoons between the East African coast and countries around the western Indian Ocean. During the early part of the nineteenth century they began to divert into the plantation economy to produce cloves for which Zanzibar has become famous. Although many members of the landowning class built their plantation houses in the countryside, the more prominent ones preferred to have their mansions in the town along the seafront to be near the Sultan's palace, or in the southern half of the peninsula which was still covered by mud huts as late as 1846.

It is said that an Englishman's home is his castle, but the Omanis extended the metaphor into reality, their home (or *beyt*) incorporating several defensive features. A typical Omani Arab house in Zanzibar was a massively built multi-story square block of coral stones and

mortar with a flat roof that was surmounted by a low crenellated wall. Most of these houses have now been capped with corrugated iron sheets to protect them from leakage in this humid climate.

These houses display elegant simplicity. The outer walls were plain and regularly punched with small windows on the upper floors, while those on the ground floor were heavily barred. The only striking external features were a few beautiful stone fretwork panels of incised stucco work that decorated some of the houses and mosques, now sadly

The Mtoni Palace was the first residence of Seyyid Said just outside the town. It was a large conglomeration of buildings which accommodated about 1,000 people. The Mtoni stream supplied it with water ending in a large pool in front of it. The centre piece was the conical wooden tower, Benjle, where the Sultan had his coffee with a full view of the sea where his fleet was anchored.

The Zanzibar sea front. It was lined by typical town houses owned by relatives of royalty and the elite who wanted to be close to the Sultan's court. Most of these houses were fairly simple on the outside, with a crenellated flat roof, small windows punctuating the barren whitewashed walls, but graced by massive carved wooden doors. External verandas were later added to some of them by British colonial officials.

A carved stone window.

defaced by constant whitewashing or disintegration of the lime plaster. More striking, however, were the elaborately carved wooden doors in a square frame (see chapter 5), decorated with iron bosses.

The Omani house was an introverted domestic structure that was influenced by the Islamic conception of privacy. It was expressed in a spiral of intimacy from the stone benches (*baraza*) that flanked the carved door at street level, where much casual social interaction took place, to the domestic quarters on the upper floors which were restricted to members of the family. The front rooms served as the reception area (*seble* or *majlis*), where the head of the household received his guests for a cup of coffee. The other rooms on the ground floor, which had little ventilation or privacy, served as servant's quarters or for storage of merchandise and produce of the plantation.

The *beyt* was organised around a central courtyard that was open to the sky, allowing

The Palace today. It was reconstructed on a smaller scale, after the 1896 bombardment and modified in 1936. It now serves as the Palace Museum.

Inside view of the Palace. Most Arab houses had a large central courtyard that was open to the sky to permit ventilation and light to penetrate the inner verandas. In due course the courtyard was roofed in many cases, as in this palace, by glass that still allowed light to come through.

An intricately cut wooden screen on the left hid the more domestic parts of the palace.

light and ventilation to penetrate the long and narrow rooms arranged around it. To veil the female members from the public gaze, broad verandas and stone arches lined the central funnel where women of the household spent much of their time attending to household chores.

In marked contrast to external plainness are the internal decorations and furnishings with which the house owners embellished their houses. We can do no better than quote from

The outer simplicity of Arab houses belies their inner beauty. They were often richly decorated with many local and imported artefacts: Local wooden chests with brass designs and tacks, used to keep clothes before cupboards became popular.

The Memoirs of an Arabian Princess about the inside of an Arab house in Zanzibar in the middle of the nineteenth century. It was written by Princess Salme who had eloped with a German businessman to Germany in the 1860s, and had written her autobiography, the first by a Zanzibari:

With rich and distinguished people, rooms are furnished more or less in the following style. Persian carpets or the finest mattings cover the floor. The whitewashed walls, which are rather thick, are always divided into several partitions by matching deep recesses which reach from floor to ceiling. The recesses are again divided by shelves of wood, painted green, forming a kind of etageren. *Upon these shelves the choicest and most expensive objects of glass and china are symmetrically arranged.*

Imported European tiles and chinaware.

A carved wooden bed in Princess Salme's Room in the Palace Museum. The room has been arranged according to her description of a typical Arab room, except for the photographs, which would have been absent.

An imported American
Regulator clock.

An Omani coffee pot.

To an Arab, nothing can be too costly to deco-
rate these recesses. A handsomely cut glass, a
beautifully painted plate, an elegant jug may
cost any price: if it only looks pretty, it is sure
to be purchased.

One also endeavours to cover the bare and
narrow walls between the recesses. Large
mirrors are placed there, reaching from the
divan, which is only slightly elevated above
the floor, to the ceiling. These mirrors are
expressly ordered from Europe. As a rule, pic-
tures, as they are imitations of Divine cre-
ation, are prohibited to a Muslim; of late,
however, they are tolerated now and then. On
the other hand, clocks are in great favour and
often the richest collection is found in any one
single house. They are placed partly over the
mirrors, partly in pairs on each side of them.

In the gentlemen's rooms the walls are decorated by trophies, consisting of all kinds of
costly weapons from Arabia, Persia and
Turkey, a decoration with which every Arab
is accustomed to adorn his house, according
to his rank and riches.

In one corner of the room is placed the
large double-bed of so-called rose-wood, very
prettily carved all over; East Indian work-
manship procures this. White muslin or tulle
covers the whole. Arab beds are very high; to
get into them easily, one first mounts upon a
chair, or makes use of the natural step of the
chambermaid's hand or that of a lady's maid.
The lofty space under the bed is often used as
sleeping-space by others, for instance by small
children's nurses or women attendants of sick
people.

Tables are rarely found, and only in the houses of the highest-placed people, but there are chairs of the most various kinds and colours. Wardrobes, chests of drawers and the like are not in use; instead, we had a sort of chest or trunk with usually two or three drawers, and inside a secret hiding place for money and jewelry. These trunks, of which there usually were several in each room, were very large, made of rosewood and beautifully adorned with thousands of small, yellow studs with brass heads.

CHAPTER 4

Indian Embellishments

Indian merchants may have been trading with the East African coast from time immemorial. The Portuguese noted Hindu traders from the Gujarat port of Cambay in Mombasa harbour in the sixteenth century. However, before the nineteenth century they do not seem to have settled permanently. In 1819 there were only 214 Indians in Zanzibar, and they complained bitterly about their weak position which allowed the Arab authorities to impose various taxes on them.

Indian merchants often started rather modestly with shopfront houses with their residential quarters at the back, to which a floor was later added. Some bought existing Arab or Swahili houses to which they added their characteristic outer verandas to increase ventilation. Later in the nineteenth century some built their houses on Indian models with elelaborate verandas skirted with intricate railings and fascia boards.

But the situation was changing rapidly in the western Indian Ocean after the end of the Anglo-French wars. As trade increased, Indian merchants found expanding opportunities there. The Omani Sultan Seyyid Said realised the potential of harnessing them to his own political and commercial ambitions in East Africa. They were accepted as full trading partners, and were given the same privileges as those granted to his Arab and Swahili subjects in the local trade. One of them even rented the revenue of the customs house for the whole East African coast for a fixed annual sum for more than half a century.

Most of the Indian merchants who came to East Africa in these early years, however, were men of limited means. Some of them were 'birds of passage', coming as single males who stayed in large dormitories (*chawls* or *maras*). They went to India when they had collected enough capital to get married. Most of their houses were plain and functional single-storied structures, lacking an inner courtyard, and exhibiting mercantile modesty. The frontage of the shop, being the most valuable part, was very narrow, only 12 to 14 feet wide. An American visitor in 1835 described them as 'mere holes raised a foot or two above the street'. The living quarters and stores were at the back of the house. These houses were arranged in narrow streets in the bazaar section of the town converging on the

market and the Custom House.

However, many Indians soon began to settle permanently and were indigenised. As they began to raise families, a second story was added to their houses, converting them into the typical shopfront houses (*uppar makan, niche dukan*, 'home above, shop below') with a four-leaf Gujarat-style door that exposed almost the whole of the front of their houses to the public. The living quarters moved to the upper floor, and elaborate windows and balconies, with delicate fretwork and coloured glazing, were often added to catch the breeze along these narrow and stuffy bazaar streets.

By 1860 whole new quarters were being

In the closely built area, some owners added a 'tea house' at the top to catch the breeze. They were used during the hot season as sleeping quarters.

The Main Road near the Post Office was lined with Indian and Goan shops before the Revolution. The street was decorated and lined with people of all races to greet the Sultan,Seyyid Khalifa bin Harub, on his silver jubilee in 1936.

established, inhabited by members of the Indian merchant class. Some bought or rented Arab houses to which they added typical Indian extrovert features. The more prosperous began to build 'large and commodious residences', reminiscent of the *haveli* of Gujarat. The windows were divided into three parts. The lower portion had a fixed panel of wrought iron and solid shutters opening outwards. The upper part had glazed shutters opening inwards and adjustable wooden louvre shutters opening outwards, allowing the breeze to flow through while cutting off the sun. These windows were generally capped by a lintel of coloured glass, throwing different colours on the inner walls.

These houses also carried intricately carved balconies which create an extension of the interior, permitting light and ventilation to penetrate the rooms and adding space for relaxation in the cool breeze. The balconies, which sometimes extended the whole length of the facade in front of the rooms on the upper story, rested on carved or decorated

The Ithna'sheri Dispensary, now the Stone Town Cultural Centre, with its double decker wooden balcony, marks the apogee of Indian-inspired architecture in Zanzibar. An artist's impression of the Dispensary before its restoration.

Tharia Topan, Indian merchant of the nineteenth century, who built it as the Jubilee Hospital in honour of Queen Victoria's golden jubilee, but did not live to see its completion.

brackets, and sometime on iron columns. They were decorated with elaborate fretwork and fascia boards cut in wood that created a pleasing play of light and shade on the facade of the house. Towards the end of the nineteenth century, these houses began to carry finely carved Indian-type doors with semi-circular lintels, modeled on the huge doors that decorated the House of Wonders. (see chapter 5).

The quest for the cool breeze in this densely built stone town in the tropics led some house owners to build higher and higher above their neighbours, and sometimes to surmount their houses with a pavilion jutting above the skyline. It provided a cool room that may have served as a tea house or a sleeping area during the hot season.

Indian architectural influence reached its apogee in the Old Dispensary, built on a grand scale by Tharia Topan, an ostentatious merchant prince, as a hospital on the occasion of Queen Victoria's Golden Jubilee. It was built at a time when Sultan Barghash was building his palaces. The front of the building consists of an ornately carved two-story balcony in which the fretwork and fascia boards run wild. The door entrances and windows as well as many parts of the interior walls are richly decorated with moulded plaster, and the large dining room on the second floor has a hook in the ceiling to hang a chandelier.

Topan died before the building could be completed, and it was bought by the trustees of Haji Nasser Nurmohamed, another prominent Indian merchant. They honoured

The front veranda overlooking the sea, with its intricate fascia boards and carvings, and the glass window with green and red colours of the Ismaili sect.

Topan's intentions (at least in part) by setting up a charitable dispensary on the ground floor, while the rest of the building was rented out as apartments to earn an income for the dispensary. The building has been recently restored to its former glory, but unfortunately the name of the institution, which had been affixed in a panel to the top of the facade, as well as the charitable intention of both benefactors, have disappeared in the process. The building now serves as the elite Stone Town Cultural Centre.

The inner balcony reminiscent of colonial India.

One manifestation of Indian settlement was the construction of multi-purpose religious complexes on a grand scale. There was at least one Hindu temple with its characteristic pointed tower by the 1870s, and there are now four. There were also some Indian Sunnis who built the ornate Hanafi mosque. Many of the Indian Muslims belonged to the minority Shi'a sects. By 1866 there were three Shi'a mosques, and by the end of the century several more were added. These complexes served not only the religious but also the social needs of the expatriate Indian communities. (see chapter 6)

The Khoja Caravanserai in the Malindi quarter of the town was built to serve short-term visitors belonging to the Ismaili sect. As immigrants, many Indian communities had such guest houses around the town for visitors, widows, etc

The interior of Indian houses were variously decorated for residential purposes. More recently some of these houses have been converted into hotels to give an exotic oriental taste.

a) The covered inner courtyard converted into a sitting room.
b) A tea-house on the top of the house serving as a recreation area.
c) A hotel room in a converted Indian mansion drenched with orientalism.
d) A bath tub in the hotel room.

A square framed door was typical of the earlier Swahili/Arab tradition

CHAPTER 5

The *Door:*
A Mark of Status & Wealth

With a subdued architecture so typical of

Zanzibar, the elaborately carved door became the most

important feature of the external appearance of a house. Its

quality and size were a mark of status and wealth of the

houseowner. As Richard Burton commented in 1857,

"the higher the tenement, the bigger the gateway, the heavier

the padlock and the huger the iron studs that nail the door of

heavy timber, the greater is the owner's dignity."

The carved Zanzibar door in an otherwise bare white-washed wall is an expression of the status of the house owner. An artist's impression brings out the richness of character and colour in the door, itself a unique piece of art.

Details of carvings highlighting various motifs of the Indian Ocean commercial world.

It was a custom for a builder first to order a carved door-frame, and then build his house around it.

There are 277 such doors in Zanzibar, the largest concentration along the Swahili coast, although they are fast diminishing as they are dismantled and sold off complete or in sections to tourists and hotel keepers.

The doors may be part of an old tradition of carving along the Swahili coast. The Portuguese writer Barbosa commented on the 'well carved' doors of Kilwa in the sixteenth century. With an abundance of wood, and an artistic maturity that can be inferred from carved coral or plaster at archaeological sites on the coast, carved doors may have been a normal part of Swahili houses. Some form of carving is present even in the simplest doors in fishing villages all over Zanzibar. The tradition may have gone into a decline during the period of Portuguese domination when Swahili commerce was fettered, but it revived towards the end of the eighteenth century, and reached its zenith during the nineteenth century with the expansion of trade and establishment of clove plantations during the period of Omani rule.

The earliest dated door of this type carries the date AH 1112 (AD1700-1) which seems unusually early in stylistic terms, and which pre-dates any other door in East Africa by more than a century. It now forms the rear door of the Peace Memorial Museum. It is said to have come from the Kidichi Palace which was built in 1832. It is possible that it came from a previous house which has now

An artist's impression of a Zanzibar door.

Details of the carving.

disappeared. It might well have acted as a prototype for the nineteenth century doors.

A typical door is square framed, often made out of termite and weather-resistant teak, imported from India or the mainland, although many are made out of local hardwoods. It is a double door that opens inwards from the centre, and a few of the larger ones have a smaller door inset within one of the shutters (or both)to allow entry without having to open the huge gates.

The normal door consists of eleven interlocking members. It firstly consists of a frame all of which is embellished by carvings, except for the treshhold. It is capped by an intricately carved lintel, and the whole is then enclosed in a carved beading to cover the joints between the wall and the door. The door also carries heavy wooden shutters which were often pivoted rather than hinged. They were traditionally plain, though inner doors were sometimes carved. Outer doors normally have iron studs across them in several lines to hold the planks together and to break the monotony of the plain wood. Finally, there is a carved centre piece which covers the junction. The door is completed with a hasp and chain to lock the door from the outside.

The carved door is one manifestation of the Indian Ocean maritime cultural region that was closely knit together by the monsoon dhows and international trade. There was constant cultural interaction in both direc-

Door carving received a big boost from commercial prosperity in the nineteenth century, becoming more massive and more intricately carved. It was embossed with pointed brass knobs. While retaining the original shape, some of the doors already betray elaborate floral designs more typical of the Indian tradition. In the door above, shutters are coffered and studded with dhow nails more typical of the Gujarat doors, although it is more elaborate.

tions between the East African coast and the northern rim of the Indian Ocean that is reflected in the decorations of the door.

Some doors carved in Pemba were imported into Oman, while others may have been imported from India to the Swahili coast, or Indian artisans were brought to Zanzibar where they have influenced the tradition.

The Zanzibar door carries a variety of motifs that highlight their maritime and mercantile context, and similar motifs appear on the elaborately carved sterns of Indian Ocean dhows. Prominent among these are the fish, fish scales and wavy lines, which point to an important source of food for the maritime Swahili people. It is generally ringed by a chain design, said to symbolise security. The lintel is decorated profusely with the rosette and the lotus flower, indicating Indian influences. Older lintels feature a Quranic inscription, and may also contain the name of the house owner or artist, and the date of carving. In some cases a whole couplet may be carved. Designs also include the frankincense and the date palm, which are indigenous to Somalia and Arabia, denoting wealth and plenty. The most beautiful piece is the central post which is carved deeply with floral and geometric motifs. It is attached to the left door shutter, called the 'female door' in Kiswahili, to which all sorts of gendered interpretations can be given.

While the rich landowners exhibited their wealth through their carved doors, Indian merchants, typical of an accumulating mercantile culture, initially preferred security and

The Indian tradition of carved doors came into its own during the last quarter of the nineteenth century when Seyyid Barghash apparently imported an Indian carver to carve his many doors in the House of Wonders. They were characterised by fleshy leaf designs, a semi-circular lintel, and the brass knobs and chain lock.

simplicity in their door design along the narrow bazaar streets. They brought with them the four-leaf Gujarat door design that exposes the whole shop front to potential customers, and sometimes a smaller side door to the domestic quarters at the back or on upper floors.

The door panels are coffered and studded with dhow nails, and the whole is often reinforced with cross bars of wood or iron at the back. The only carved portions of the door in the more ornate ones were the projecting corbels at the upper corners, and a modest centre post carved with rosettes and floral designs. Greater flourish was exhibited in the lintel which consisted of a flowing fleshy leaf design interspersed with rosettes, sometimes with an oval plaque containing the name of the owner and date. Interestingly, however, even on houses owned by Hindus, the inscription was sometimes in Arabic, and may even have a Qur'anic verse, suggesting carving by local Muslim artisans.

During the latter part of the nineteenth century, coinciding with the opulence and ostentation associated with the reign of Seyyid Barghash (1870-1888), there was a fresh and heavy Indian influence on Zanzibar architecture. Barghash had been exiled to Bombay in 1860 after his failed rebellion against his brother, and he was immensely impressed by the splendours of the British Raj. He tried to emulate them when he became Sultan of Zanzibar. He built a large number of palaces, including the Beit al-Ajaib (House of Wonders). Built in 1883, it has 13

These doors take their inspiration from the front door of the House of Wonders and a couple of others, obviously carved by the same person. They carry unusual animal carvings on the centre post. Representation of animate objects is forbidden in Islam, and most house owners deleted this feature in their doors, such as that in the house of Tippu Tip, the pioneer Arab trader of eastern Congo who retired to a life of settled luxury in the Stone Town.

carved doors, the largest in Zanzibar. They provided models for subsequent developments of the Zanzibar door.

These doors usually have a semi-circular lintel filled with intricate foliate carving that is sometimes perforated, allowing light to pass through. The centre of the lintel may be occupied by a shield design carrying a Qur'anic inscription, name and date, or a floral vase design. While the carved frame in typical doors was squared, in the new design it was often rounded with flowing floriate patterns around the posts, and the sides of the door frame sometimes took the shape of classical pillars. Even the thresholds of these doors were sometimes carved. The centre post was also very elaborate with rosette patterns, and in the original three doors, which were obviously carved by the same Indian artisan (if not imported fully decorated) the top of the post contains finely carved animal figures, unusual embellishments in an austere Muslim culture. Finally, the door shutters are studded with pointed brass bosses, decorative adaptation of ancient defences against the battering war-elephants, and the door was completed with an ornamental chain lock.

Such doors are concentrated in the newer southern section of the town in Shangani and Baghani quarters which were settled by members of the rich Omani landowners including the famous Tipu Tip and Indian merchants. However, the animal designs on the centre pieces were generally not reproduced in them.

The inner doors on the upper floors of the

Beit al-Ajaib are carved in a unique rococo style. The green frames are carved in gilt geometrical and floral designs, and in a few cases end with lions in brass at the foot of the posts. Both sides of the doors are covered with texts from the Qur'an, arranged in geometrical designs on the front, and across the shutters in straight lines at the back. The texts, which were designed by a local calligrapher, were cut in wood and nailed to the shutters, thus standing out in relief.

After the Revolution of 1964, the art of door carving almost died. The commercial revival since the mid 1980s, however, has brought it back to life, and a new generation of carvers has been trained.

The Revolution of 1964 had a disastrous effect upon the architectural heritage of the Stone Town. With the departure of many Arab and Indian owners of Stone Town houses, they began to collapse. In 1983 the Habitat Report on the Stone Town asserted that 'the craft of making the carved doors is now almost extinct, and it may be unrealistic to try to revive the tradition on a scale sufficient for new construction.' The foremost door carver, Maalim Yahya, had moved to Dar es Salaam where he was carving furniture for expatriates.

But the art, and its habitat the Stone Town, refuse to die. With trade liberalisation in the mid 1980s, both have been given a new lease of life. Every house owner and builder of hotels now wants a carved door to grace his structure. Maalim Yahya returned and was put in charge of the woodwork section in the Mikunguni Trades School. He has now trained a whole new generation of Zanzibari woodcarvers of both sexes who are fortunately proving Habitat's pessimism wrong.

The 'mihrab' of the twelfth century mosque at Kizimkazi, with its unique Kufic inscription, has acted as a prototype for many later mosques.

CHAPTER 6

Mosques, Churches & Temples:
A Gathering of World Religions

Consistent with its cosmopolitan character, Zanzibar has always offered a very high degree of religious tolerance to all its citizens. The Stone Town is thus a gathering of world religions, with 48 mosques, four Hindu temples, a Zoroastrian Fire temple, a Buddhist temple, and two Christian cathedrals.

The minaret is usually associated with mosques, but in Zanzibar they are not common. Some mosques, however, do have unique minarets.

a) The conical minaret of the Bamnara mosque.
b) An elaborately designed minaret of the Hanafi mosque of the Indian Sunni population in Kajificheni.
c) A tall minaret has been recently added to an old Ibadhi mosque which otherwise lacked such ostentation.

The predominant religion of Zanzibar is Islam. The oldest mosque on the East African coast, still in use, is at Kizimkazi, 58 km south of the Stone Town. It was built in AD 1107 and is graced by a unique floriate Kufic script carved in porite coral that may have been inspired by the Siraf school in the Persian Gulf. It has a trefoil arch over the *mihrab* (the prayer niche) which seems to have acted as a model for many nineteenth century mosques in the Stone Town.

In the Stone Town itself the oldest mosque is the Malindi Bamnara Mosque dating to the seventeenth century. Its unique elliptical minaret may have been inspired by the tall minarets in south-western Arabia. The only other remarkable minaret is that on the Shi'a mosque at Hamamni with a pronounced Indian architectural influence. Minarets, which elsewhere are so typical of Islamic architecture, are rather rare in Zanzibar, although many have begun to built in recent years. The more common form was a stair-case minaret to the roof of the mosque from where the call to prayers is made.

Most of the mosques in Zanzibar are fairly plain on the outside, hardly distinguishable from domestic buildings except for the pro-trusion of the *kibla* (direction of the mosque)

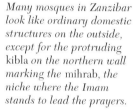

Many mosques in Zanzibar look like ordinary domestic structures on the outside, except for the protruding kibla *on the northern wall marking the* mihrab, *the niche where the Imam stands to lead the prayers.*

a) Entrance to a simple mosque dating to the mid nineteenth century.
b) With the expansion of the Barza mosque in Mkunazini a new kibla was added without demolishing the original one, making it a mosque with two kiblas.

on the north side. This, as well as the absence of minarets, may be due to the influence of the puritanical Ibadhi sect of the ruling class. They frowned upon any architectural embellishments in the House of God which might detract worshippers from their prayers.

Sunni Muslims, however, were less restrained when it came to internal decoration, centred particularly on the *mihrab*, the prayer leader's niche, though they were still disciplined. The Stone Town mosques show a great variety of mihrab designs and internal arches to support the thick ceiling. Although the skill exhibited by Swahili masons was not uniformly high, the old mosques show a unity of style that modern builders have great difficulty in maintaining.

Elegant simplicity in mosque design is even more marked in Ibadhi mosques. Many of them were small since they were built for the family or clan, and they were generally broad

and shallow so as to allow as many people as possible to say their prayers in the first two rows, a practice which was considered meritorious. The mosques were often raised a metre or more above street level, raising worshippers above the din or disturbance of the street. The *mihrab* is ideally entirely plain and shallow, contained within the thickness of the wall, so that the *kibla* does not protrude from the north wall. However, some form of decoration was sometimes tolerated, as in the Mtoni mosque which has a beautiful *mihrab*-within-a-*mihrab* design that was directly imported from Oman. Some of these mosques also have beautiful stone fretwork to allow ventilation and light into the mosques.

The Ibadhi mosque in Zanzibar, however, was not simply a place of worship, but also in some sense a community centre for an immigrant minority. Although most mosques serve as centres of religious education as well, Ibadhi mosques specifically provided for a *madrasa* (religious school) behind the courtyard where young children could be taught the Qur'an and Traditions of the Prophet. As

c) The Jum'a mosque at Mizingani, the biggest in the Stone Town, expanded in the 1940s, and recently refurbished, with a large courtyard in front to cater for the overflow during the Friday prayers.
d) The front gate to the Ithna'sheri mosque at Kiponda capped with a platform, presumably to serve as a minaret, but neither have been used as such.

e) The main entrance to the Ismaili Jamatkhana with a carved Gujarat-style door and brass knobs, bearing the inscription of the benefactor who rebuilt it at the beginning of the twentieth century.

The mihrab from where the Imam leads the prayers, is the most central part of the mosque. The Barza mosque at Mkunazini which is very broad but very shallow, admitting only three rows of worshippers at are time.

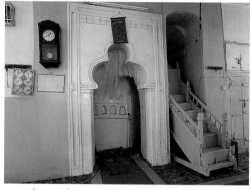

The mimbar or pulpit from where the Imam presented his sermon. In this case a movable mimbar that can be pushed in to allow a full use of the mosque during prayers.

The brightly lit mihrab in a Bohora mosque, with carved wooden pillars supporting an upper floor. Women were accommodated on the upper floor. They could listen to the sermons through a large opening in the centre.

Ablution is essential before entering a mosque. All the mosques have such facilities at the back of the building where the faithful may wash their feet, arms and faces.

members of a migrant community, they also provided modest accommodation for the visiting merchant and scholar during the monsoons in a room next to the *madrasa*.

This concept of a multi-purpose community centre becomes even more pronounced in the case of mosques belonging to the Indian communities. For immigrants belonging to various minority Shi'a sects, mosques also served as nodes of social solidarity. They had to provide for social as well as religious needs. These complexes, therefore, included not only the place of worship, but also a place for religious sermons (*majlis*), communal feasts, offices for the community organisation, and so on. Although most of the mosques in Zanzibar were for men only, with women saying their prayers at home, in Shi'a mosques space was set aside for women to take part in other religious and social functions behind a partition or on an upper floor, sometimes with an opening in the floor to enable them to hear the sermon. These mosques naturally show a heavy Indian architectural influence in

The roofs of many of the older mosques were supported by double polylobed arches.

their carving and decorations, and the halls are often full of chandeliers and lights which would be absent from Ibadhi and Sunni mosques.

Indian architectural influence is naturally much more pronounced in Hindu temples, complete with their characteristic pointed towers, one of which was established in Zanzibar as early as the 1870s. The main temple lies behind the Palace Museum completely surrounded by houses with the painted towers just barely jutting above them. In addition to this temple there are other smaller chapels in some houses along the bazaar streets hardly identifiable from the outside, and a Vedic temple at the north-east corner of the Old Fort.

The latter half of the nineteenth century saw increasing European influence in East Africa, accompanied by growing missionary interest, epitomised by the tall towers of the Anglican and Roman Catholic cathedrals which pierce the Stone Town sky. The Anglican effort was spearheaded by David Livingstone who inspired the formation of the Universities' Mission to Central Africa (UMCA) and was closely associated with the anti-slavery crusade. The Anglican Cathedral has capitalised on all the symbolism associated with its new mission, but it also represents an attempt to integrate it into the Zanzibari society.

The foundation stone was laid in 1873, the year in which all slave trade by sea was abolished, but the site on which it was built was donated by the Indian farmer of customs,

Hindus enjoyed complete freedom of beliefs since the nineteenth century when the first temples were constructed.

The Hindu temple with three towers just behind the palace of the Sultan.

The prayer chamber in the Vedic Arya Samaj temple behind the Old Fort.

*Page 68 and 69:
Entrance to the temple, complete with the representation of the holy cow and a statue of the Hindu god.*

and as a sign of royal goodwill, the clock in the tower was presented by Sultan Barghash. The construction was supervised by Bishop Steere who used Portland cement and coral stones as well as local masons, and he combined Gothic and Arabic architectural features. The roof has a span of nearly nine metres and stands at a height of 18 metres, and the church can seat 600 people. The altar stands where the whipping-post of the old slave market is said to have been, and the crucifix on the north wall is made of wood taken from the tree at Chitambo in Zambia where Livingstone's heart was buried.

There was an active effort by the Anglican bishops to win over Muslims. There used to be a gallery for the use of woman wearing the Muslim veil, which is now used as a chapel, and in another adjoining the Cathedral, Bishop Steere used to address Muslims every Friday. Relations between the two world religions seem to have been cordial, but few

St. Joseph's Roman Catholic Cathedral built towards the end of the nineteenth century.

Detail of the painting on the dome.

The altar, with painting of the prophets all around and on the dome.

seem to have converted to Christianity.

The Roman Catholic mission was inaugurated in 1860 by the Abe' Fava, Vicar-General of the French Indian Ocean island of Reunion. The Cathedral was designed in Romanesque style by M. Berangier, the architect of Notre Dame de la Garde of Marseilles. Over the main entrance is a group of statues, and the interior is painted throughout with religious motifs from the Old Testament which now require urgent attention. The first mass was celebrated in this Cathedral on Christmas night, 1898.

The Stone Town is thus a heterogeneous urban environment even in religious terms. People belonging to a multiplicity of religions and sects lived in the town, concentrated to some extent around their religious institutions, but they also participated in the celebrations of each other's festivals, such as Eid, Diwali and Christmas. Though some of the religious institutions publicly portrayed statues and expressed beliefs that were anathema to the majority Muslims, and though some were directly associated with European expansionism and the resulting (and sometimes painful) social dislocations, they were all accommodated within the tolerant cosmopolitan milieu. The history of Zanzibar has had some periods of tension and crises, but it is remarkable that none of the major conflicts in this multi-religious society have been sectarian.

*1880s. In the centre is Beit al-Hukm built by
Seyyid Majid. The building to the left is Beit al-Sahel, the old palace which was
refurbished by Seyyid Barghash, who also built Beit al-Ajaib on the right. These
palaces, and many others in the area, were connected by covered galleries
(vikio), permitting passage from one to the other without having to come down to
street level.*

CHAPTER 7

Bargash:
"Harun Rashid of the Busaidis"

Of all the Omani rulers of Zanzibar, Seyyid Barghash bin Said (1870-1888) left the most indelible mark on its architecture. He has been described as the 'Harun Rashid of the Busaidis' after the great Caliph of Baghdad. He was a great builder of palaces and public facilities.

The Chukwani palace to the south of the town, built by Seyyid Barghash in the 1870s. The influence of colonial India is very apparent.

His eighteen-year reign was squeezed between two calamitous events that Zanzibar suffered during the nineteenth century. He was hardly on the throne when Zanzibar was struck by a terrible hurricane in 1872 and the slave trade was abolished in 1873. The former had wrecked many of the houses in the town and shipping in the harbour, and it all but wiped out its valuable clove plantations. The abolition of the slave trade deprived plantation owners of the vital labour force. On the other hand, towards the end of his reign Barghash could do little to stop the Scramble for Africa of the 1880s which partitioned his commercial empire on the African mainland among the hungry powers of Europe, thus cutting off Zanzibar from its valuable hinterland. Nevertheless, in the intervening period, Barghash did much not only for his own com-

The Marhubi palaces to the north of the town, built by Seyyid Barghash in the 1880s.

fort, but also for the comfort of his subjects.

During his reign Zanzibar reached its peak as a commercial centre of eastern Africa. It was connected to the world of commerce by underwater telegraph cables, and after the opening of the Suez Canal in 1869, it became a regular stopping point for all steamers. He supplemented them with six steamers of his own which he ordered from Germany to ply between Zanzibar, Aden and Bombay, on which he provided free passage pilgrims to go to Mecca. As a result, state revenues increased four-fold during his reign.

The inflow of wealth allowed him to embark on a massive programme of construction of many palaces in the town and country. He had been greatly impressed by the splendours of the Indian princes during his exile in Bombay in 1860, and those of the

The House of Wonders was much influenced by colonial architecture in India. Originally it had a plain roof. It was slightly damaged in the 1896 bombardment which, however, destabilised the lighthouse that used to stand separately in front. It was demolished, and a tower was added to the House of Wonders to give it its present shape.

West during his visit to Europe in 1875. He built the Chuini Palace in 1872 on an artificial foundation in a river bed to allow water to flow through its many baths into the sea, but it burned down in 1914. He built the Chukwani Palace on a promontory commanding a magnificent view of the sea. The Marhubi Palace was built in 1880-82 surrounded by a wall that was inspired by the park walls in England. One of its features was an avenue of Indian mangoes, leading to large water lily ponds. Stone aqueducts supplied the palace and its many baths with

water from the Chem Chem spring. The palace is said to have been the most charming of all, with stairs of black and white marble leading to a large balcony supported on big round stone pillars. It was accidentally burnt down in 1899. These country palaces were connected to the town by telephone in the 1880s, and Chukwani was served by a light tram.

The pride of his palaces, however, was the Beit al-Ajaib (House of Wonders) on the seafront in Zanzibar town. It was built in 1883 for ceremonial purposes. It is an enormous

The palaces were lavishly furbished with chandeliers and clocks, imported from Europe, and furniture from Europe and British India.

a) The huge chandeliers in the Palace survived the bombardment of 1896, as can still be seen in the Palace Museum, although many of the huge mirrors and furniture were badly damaged.
b) The lovers' sofa on which partners could sit face to face. It seems to be of British Indian origin. It has been preserved in the Palace Museum in Zanzibar.

square block based on the typical Omani design, with rooms lining the four sides of the building and broad verandas around the central funnel. Wide galleries were added to the outer walls, supported by massive cast-iron pillars imported from England. The view from there of the harbour and the rest of the town is simply breath-taking.

The Wonders of the House, however, did not lie so much in the mass of the relatively simple structure, as in the decorations that went into it. The most prominent were the huge carved doors that embellished it at every level. The main door is intricately carved with animal motifs which are unusual in a house belonging to a puritanical Muslim ruler. The door also has a heavily carved semi-circular lintel that was introduced from India at that time, and it inaugurated a new tradition in door carving. The other doors on the upper floors carry elaborate floriate designs, with texts of the Qur'an painted in gilt on a green background.

The House was paved with black and white marble slabs imported from Europe, and majestic staircases in teak coil up from one floor to another. It was exquisitely illuminated by huge chandeliers, powered in 1886 by an electric power generator, the first in sub-Saharan Africa. This also provided light to other palaces, consulates and houses on the seafront. The palace was furnished with beautifully carved furniture in ebony, and Persian carpets covered the floors. Seyyid Ali bin Humoud used the House briefly as a residential palace, and he had a sitting room in fretted cedar and teak on the second floor. In the court in front of the House there were lions and other animals in cages, presents to the sultan, that no doubt added to the awe that the House of Wonders inspired among the inhabitants of the town.

While the court of Seyyid Barghash was no doubt lavish, his interest was not confined to his palaces. Perhaps the greatest bequest to his people was the supply of fresh water to the town to reduce their dependence on the highly contaminated wells, as expressed in the still current names of some of the wards, such as Kisimamajongoo (the well of the millipedes), Kisiwa Ndui (the smallpox island). Stone aqueducts were constructed from Chem Chem springs a few kilometres north of the town, and their remains can still be

The Boat Water Tank. Provision of potable water to the town from a spring outside the town was considered such an important public work by Seyyid Barghash that he built the tank from where the public could fetch their water right in front of his Palace. In the background is the old lighthouse.

The Public Hammam (Persian steam bath) in the middle of the town, built by Seyyid Barghash for the public, apart from smaller ones in many of the palaces he built.

The Hammam consisted of a utility area around a water pool where visitors could have a shave or massage, a cold and hot steam bath, and toilets.

seen at Saateni. Large iron pipes distributed water throughout the town. A huge water tank in the shape of a ship was built in front of the palace where citizens could come to fetch water. He bequeathed the Darajani Chawl (commercial-cum-residential complex) for the maintenance of the water system. Water was supplied free of charge to the people, and there has been considerable resistance to the imposition of rates on this essential social service in Zanzibar.

Apart from the Persian baths in his various palaces, Barghash also built a Persian steam bath at Hamamni in the centre of the town for use by the general public. It was designed by a Persian Haji Ghulamhusain who had also designed the beautiful baths at the Kidichi palace north of the town which has intricate

The Victoria Garden, originally laid out by Seyyid Barghash for recreation of his harem. It was offered to the public and named after the British queen by Seyyid Humoud towards the end of the nineteenth century.

The roof of the Hammam with the domes protruding above the surface.

floral and animal motifs. The Hamamni baths are on a larger scale, divided into the utility area, the cold fountain, and the hot baths.

Barghash also laid out what later became the Victoria Gardens for the use of his harem, complete with baths which have now been covered over. It was given over to the public by Seyyid Humoud, and a botanical garden was established with plants from Sir John Kirk's collection at his house at Mbweni. The pavilion in the garden was later used as the Legislative Council during the colonial period, and it has now been restored to serve, incongruously, as the Sewerage Department.

'Harun Rashid of the Busaidis' has indeed left a permanent imprint on the architecture of Zanzibar. The ship water tank has disappeared, but Barghash's gift of water still resides in the memory of many older inhabitants. Most of his palaces are now in ruins, but the Beit al-Ajaib which will house, appropriately, the new Zanzibar Museum of History & Culture, still stands as a sentinel watching over the harbour of Zanzibar.

The High Court with its characteristic dome, the clock and the moorish arch.

CHAPTER 8

"Sinclarian Saracenism*"*

In 1890 Zanzibar became a British Protectorate. This was the age of indirect rule, designed to make colonialism palatable. The British, therefore, retained the Sultan as a figurehead, complete with ceremonial robes and turban. In that same spirit they tried to blend the new colonial architecture into the existing styles of Zanzibar. In fact they did more than that, for they tried to orientalise the formerly subdued Zanzibari architecture by introducing or exaggerating 'Saracenic' or Arabic features, especially the arches and the domes.

The State House, formerly the British Residency, with its perforated polylobed Moorish arches.

The catalytic figure in this development was a young colonial officer who came to Zanzibar in 1896 at the age of 25. John Sinclair had been a pupil of J. L. Pearson, the architect of a number of churches in England. He used his training in designing the stalls and pulpit of the Anglican Cathedral in Zanzibar. But his main architectural inspiration seems to have come from the Muslim world, from Istanbul and Morocco, and he has left a rich legacy in Zanzibar and all over East Africa.

During his 27-year career in Zanzibar he designed a large number of public and private buildings that established an architectural tradition in its own right. Among the first was the British Residency which was built in 1903. It has a number of polylobed arches similar to those found in many mosques in Zanzibar. The building was embellished with typical Moorish arches that can also be seen in the High Court, and crenellation partially hiding the tiled roof. The High Court also has a large round dome capped by a gilded ring, a typical Islamic motif, by which it was believed, sanctified buildings will be lifted to heaven, but the ring has unfortunately disappeared.

Sinclair designed a number of other humbler buildings, including the Post Office in the Stone Town, the old Majestic Cinema, which burnt down in the 1950s, and its twin, the Institute of Kiswahili & Foreign Languages, and of course his own house on the beach at Maisara Grounds.

In 1915 he designed Kassrusaada Palace

The Institute of Kiswahili and Foreign Languages, formerly the Aga Khan Secondary School, with its two domes, resembled the more ornate old Majestic Cinema which was burnt down in the 1950s.

(Palace of Happiness) for Seyyid Khalifa at Kibweni. He capped his career in Zanzibar with a spectacular building. For the Peace Memorial Museum building, which was completed in 1925 after his retirement, he drew inspiration from the Aya Sophia Mosque in Istanbul, with six hexagonal domes supporting a huge dome in the centre. In the same spirit is the Bharmal Building, buit in 1923 for an Indian merchant, with elaborate coloured glass windows and plaster moulding reminis-

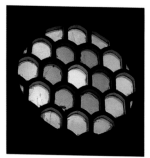

The Peace Memorial Museum, built in memory of the dead in the First World war, designed on the model of the Aya Sophia Mosque in Istanbul. It has beautiful coloured glass panels to light up the exhibition hall, and gracefully barred arched windows.

cent of colonial India.

Apart from these architectural land-marks, as in their other colonial teritories the new rulers established a European quarter for its colonial officials in the southern half of the peninsula at Vuga and Mji Mpya. The huts which then covered the area were cleared out and replaced by low density bungalow-com-

pound residences for British officials, with
low garden walls shaded by trees, giving the
impression of a transplanted European
suburb.

Sinclair's legacy is not confined to Zanzibar.
He designed the Cathedral and other govern-
ment buildings in Mombasa, and the State
House in Dar es Salaam when it was recon-

Gracefully barred arched windows of the Peace Memorial Museum.

Bharmal Building on the Creek Road, built for an Indian merchant, with more pronounced colonial Indian architectural features, including moulded stucco and coloured glass windows

structed after the First World War, reminiscent of the State House in Zanzibar, but on a much larger scale. He ultimately retired to Tangier, the home of his architectural inspiration, but his influence on Zanzibar did not end. He was invited to be a consultant for Colonial Development and Welfare projects in Zanzibar after the Second World War. A large number of schools and other public buildings were constructed carrying his Moorish trade mark, and overseen by an admiring successor as Chief Secretary, Major E. A. T. Dutton.

Among these buildings were new housing for colonial officials at Mazizini, but not everybody was happy with 'Saracenic' architecture. As one colonial official says in his memoirs:

In Zanzibar all plans for new buildings had to be vetted by the Chief Secretary, whose hobby was architecture. It was his no doubt excellent conception that all modern buildings in Zanzibar must conform to a style which he caused to be known as 'Neosaracenic'. This was considered to be the appropriate manner for an Arab city. It involved the construction of maddeningly Moorish arches, of lattice-work balustrades and pointed architraves, of turrets, domes and cupolas reminiscent of old Baghdad.... Thus the new Maternity Hospital ... assumed the aspect of a Caliph's palace. A cinema near the docks seemed to have affinities with the Alhambra, while the new airport building seemed to have exchanged nods with the Great Mosque at Cairo. 2

2. F.d. ommaney, isle of cloves, London, 1957, page 86

This is highly exaggerated, but looking at
the alternative flat concrete boxes that have
been prevalent since the 1950s, we are thankful that Sinclair's Saracenic inspiration has
cast such a benevolent shadow for so long.

The heavy rains, and neglect, has led to a serious deterioration of the Stone Town over the past thirty years. The child is surveying the decay around him.

CHAPTER 9

Epilogue: Decay and Rejuvention

*The partition of its hinterland on the African mainland
between the various colonial powers, and the abolition of
slavery dealt a severe blow to the commercial and plantation
economy of Zanzibar. They also affected the fortunes of the
landowners and merchants who inhabited the Stone Town, as
well as the working class that had depended on that economy. The town therefore stagnated, but it did not die.*

The lone street lamp looks down sadly, no longer able to light up the street at night.

The Revolution of 1964, however, brought about dramatic social and economic upheaval to Zanzibar. The nationalisation of the clove economy and many of the houses hit at the very heart of the inhabitants of the town who where driven by fear and economic hardship to migrate to the Tanzanian mainland and beyond . The population of the Stone Town declined by 15% in 20 years, and the population itself was turned inside out as the departing citizens were replaced by others from the rural areas, driven there by economic hardship into an unfamiliar urban situation. By 1992 less than half of the population of the stone town was indigenous to it.

With nationalisation more than 60% of the houses came into the hands of the government, and the former extended family houses were partitioned and rented out to low-income residents. Neither the goverment nor the new occupants had the means or desire to maintain the old houses. The result was decay. More than 85% of the houses are at various stages of deterioration; more than 100 houses have collapsed altogether, and every rainy season adds to that number.

With the change in the economic policies since the mid 1980s, there has been a change in the fortune of the Stone Town.

Government attitude has changed towards the Stone Town which is now considered a valuble national heritage that can attract toursim. A Stone Town Conservation and Development Authority has been set up, and the necessary legislation has been passed to preserve the town. There has also been a

renewal of confidence in the future of the town among those with the means to repair their old houses.

A tree growing out of the wall made up of stone and mud.

There are signs of revival, but the change, and the furious pace at which it is proceeding, is threatening to do as much damage as previous neglect. The *nouveau riche* and the over-mighty foreign investors are not always in tune with the heartbeat of the old Stone Town. Repairs carried out with inappropriate materials, and inappropriate modifications to suit the exotic needs of the tourism industry alienate the restored houses from the culture of the Stone Town. The town is not only a collection of buildings, but the sum total of human relations developed over the past two centuries, and perhaps longer. The Stone Town has seen many phases of change in its lifetime; it needs change, but one that is in line with its spirit.

Dhow sailing near the coast.

Useful Readings

Habitat, 1983, <u>The Stone Town of Zanzibar: A Strategy for Integrated Development,</u> U.N. Center for Human Settlement, Washington.

Jafferji, Javed, 1996, <u>Images of Zanzibar,</u> HSP Publications, London.

Ruete, Emily, 1989, <u>Memoirs of an Arabian Princess from Zanzibar,</u> with an Introduction by P.W. Romero, Markus Weiner, Princeton.

Salme, Sayyida, (Emily Reute), 1993, <u>An Arabian Princess Between Two Worlds,</u> ed. With an Introduction by E.Van Donzel, E.J. Brill, Leiden.

Siravo, Francesco., 1998, <u>Zanzibar: A Plan for the Historic Stone Town,</u> The Gallery Publications, Zanzibar.

Sheriff, Abdul,. 1987, <u>Slaves, Spices and Ivory in Zanzibar,</u> James Curry, London. 1987.

,ed. 1993, <u>History & Conservation of Zanzibar Stone Town,</u> James Currey, London. 1993.

1996, <u>Historical Zanzibar-Romance of the Ages,</u> Introduction by A. Sheriff, HSP Publications, London. 1996.

,and Ed Ferguson, eds., 1991, <u>Zanzibar Under Colonial Rule,</u> James Curry, London.

<u>Zanzibar Guide,</u> 1994, HSP Publications, London.

Mcthcin, Mame,. 1998, <u>Zanzibar-An Essential Guide.</u> The Gallery Publications, Zanzibar.

If you would like to get details of our new publications, please send your name and address on a postcard to:The Gallery Publications P.O.Box 3181, Zanzibar.